FAITH-CHAT PLATFORM HANDBOOK

Understanding the Catholic Doctrines and Catechisms

Acknowledgement

Faith-Chat Platform is grateful to God, to our director Fr. James Anyaegbu, to our erudite contributors, to our formidable Outreach volunteer team and all members of our group.

We are nothing without one another! Thank you!

Understanding the Catholic Doctrines and Catechisms

Published in the United Kingdom
by Sapphire Publishing, an imprint
of Sapphire Media & Entertainment, Ltd.,
71-75 Shelton Street, Covent Garden,
London, WC2H 9JQ.

Book design by Kateryna Barbina

ISBN (paperback): 978-1-909536-13-5
ISBN (hardcover): 978-1-909536-18-0

Contents

About Faith-chat Platform 6
Introduction 9
Contributors 11

BAPTISM

Why Does the Catholic Church Baptise Infants and Children Below the Age of Consent? 12

HOLY EUCHARIST

What is the Holy Eucharist, and Can a Non-catholic Christian Receive the Holy Eucharist? 17

MASS

How is Mass a Prayer? 20

CONFIRMATION

What is the Difference Between the Anointing at Baptism and Confirmation? 23

PENANCE

Why Do Catholics Confess to Their Priests? 26

Can Confession Be Done Online or Through Third-party Means? 30

What is the Difference Between Mortal Sin and Venial Sin? 33

What is Indulgence and How Can One Receive It? 36

EXTREME-UNCTION

What Happens if a Catholic Dies Without the Sacrament of Extreme Unction/anointing of the Sick? 39

HOLY ORDERS
Ministerial Priesthood Versus Ordinary Priesthood 42
MARRIAGE
Can a Catholic Marry a Non-catholic Partner in the Catholic Church? 48
Why is Divorce Not Accepted in the Church? 51
SALVATION
Is There Salvation Apart From Christ? 54
PURGATORY
Why Do Catholics Believe in Purgatory? 57
SAINTS
Why Do Catholics Pray for the Dead and to the Dead (Saints)? 59
MARY
How is Mary the Mother of God?. 61
SACRED TRADITION
What is Sacred Tradition and Why Do Catholics Believe in It? 65
Why Do Catholics Use Images Against God's Command? 68
Why is the Catholic Bible Different From Protestant and Pentecostal Bibles? 71
References 74

About Faith-chat Platform

Faith-Chat Platform, as the name implies, is a platform for the enlightenment of young Catholic Christians and for practical charity. The Platform was founded by Fr. James Anyaegbu as an apposite response to the contemporary crisis of faith. With the question, *"But when the Son of man comes, will he find any faith on earth?"* (Luke 18:8). The brisk metamorphosis of the crisis of faith in the world of today is in sync with the swift trend of technological advancement, where the internet and social media seem to have gained primacy. This primacy is not unconnected to a manner of frenzy, wherein the fastest relay runner is approaching the finishing line with no baton in hand. But then the frenzy is not all about gloom since it could be moderately approached and explored in order to bring out the beauty and at the same time project that which is needed to properly live out the faith. In the spirit of aggiornamento (to bring up to date), the challenges of an advanced generation necessarily call for advanced solution, *"otherwise the new wine will not blend with the old wineskin"* (Matthew 9:17).

Today, the new trend of our modern society is social media, which has attained the status of a culture. It has become virtually impossible to wade through the media without stumbling across something that cast doubts on one's faith or something that discourages one's doctrinal standpoint.

The Faith-Chat Platform is there to respond to those who may not have had strong parental or ecclesial upbringing in matters of faith; but it is also an avenue to help those who are having material challenges. It is as well a platform for those who feel that the Catholic Church has failed them. Here, their disquietude and quietness are listened to even as opportunity is offered to them to express their doubts, weaknesses and worries. On the Faith-Chat Platform, these brothers and sisters draw strength from the stories and experiences of others with a stronger understanding of the teachings of the Catholic Church.

We are founded on two wings that fly simultaneously: "The Word/Prayer and Practical Charity".

Word/Prayer: We start each month with prayers accompanied by monthly Novenas. Every Monday we pray the Holy Rosary; we read and reflect on the Scriptures, the Catechism of the Church and other spiritual books. We organise talks and discussions on modern trends and how they affect our faith with themes such as — marriage, the new understanding of modesty and virtues as against modern vices, Internet safety, and self-esteem.

We organise most of our prayer sessions online mainly through Instagram Live, then sometimes on TikTok and Facebook. Usually at 7am (UK & Nigerian time), this time varies in different countries but to our astonishment, there are people who would wake up at midnight in their time zones to join our prayers and participate in our bible sessions.

Practical Charity: We promote life as a relationship to be lived in love, this is the reason we have as one of our phrases: *Made by love, in love and for love.* We feel we have a responsibility to the poor. St. Camillus de Lellis says: "*The poor and the sick are the hearts of God and in serving them, we serve Jesus*". We aim at giving hope to the hopeless.

We have so far visited care homes, orphanages, slums, hospitals and prisons located in various countries in Africa. Our target is to move 5000 children off the streets by offering them educational opportunities. To ensure we do not just give bread, we also aim to teach the youth how to bake them. We empower young and unemployed people by organising skill acquisitions programs and we assist them set up a small / medium enterprise.

Our funds are from benevolent men and women of good will and institutions willing to make a change in our world. We have a formidable team of volunteers comprised of young and professional ladies and gentlemen.

Feel free to join us; let us, as one, make some little positive change in our world today!

Introduction

> *"Neither graces, nor revelations, nor raptures, nor gifts granted to a soul make it perfect, but the intimate union of the soul with God"* (St. Maria Faustina Kowalska).

The soul gains this union through knowledge and practice of the various spiritual teachings, doctrines, and traditions of the Christian faith. Knowledge is information we obtain through teaching or experiences, the knowledge that results when we listen to a Christ witness, is called Faith.

> *"Faith comes from hearing, and hearing through the word of Christ"* (Romans 10:17).

This book is a witness to the truth of faith, it contains the fundamental teachings and doctrines of our Christian faith. Some of the teachings addressed in this book are born out of the many questions that have consistently featured during Faith-Chat Platform meetings. Examples of these are: understanding infant Baptism, Purgatory, Eucharist, Divorce, Mary as the Mother of God and Sacraments as means to salvation.

While non-Catholic believers reject the doctrine that sacraments are means to salvation, the Catholic Church affirms that the sacraments of the New Covenant are necessary for salvation. The Catechism of the Catholic Church was clear about the sacraments as the

> *"efficacious signs of grace, instituted by Christ and entrusted to the Church by which divine life is dispensed to us. They are outward signs of inward grace, instituted by Christ to help individuals in their spiritual life and to grow in holiness"* (CCC 1131).

Many Catholics are afraid to be faced with questions about their faith because they may not have the right answers for them. Some are unable to openly profess their faith and doctrinal beliefs in order to avoid awkward encounters. It is our hope that the words and teachings presented in this book, can help you completely trust God and prepare you to defend your faith when necessary.

Understanding the Catholic Doctrines and Catechism is the first book in the series of the Faith-Chat Platform's handbooks. These handbooks will be presented with powerful, absorbing and life changing teachings and messages to educate you and serve as a lamp to illumine your days.

Contributors

This book has been made possible through the written contributions of the following people:

Rev. Fr. Boniface Nkem Anusiem (PhD)
Rev. Fr. Emmanuel Bekomson
Rev. Fr. Emmanuel Omokugbo Ojeifo (PhD)
Rev. Fr. Gabriel Emeasoba (PhD)
Rev. Fr. James Anyaegbu
Rev. Fr. Johnpromise Umeozuru
Friar JudeMary Owoh (OP)
Rev. Fr. Kelvin Ugwu (MSP)
Rev. Fr. Maximilian Nwosu
Rev. Fr. Paschal Okpaleke (PhD)
Friar Paul Orerhime Akpomie (OP)
Rev. Fr. Ugochukwu Ugwoke (ISch)

Special thanks to Sandra Michael for compiling the written contributions.

BAPTISM

Why Does the Catholic Church Baptise Infants and Children Below the Age of Consent?

Rev. Fr. James Anyaegbu

Infant baptism has been a practice for many centuries, it was not explicit in the New Testament but when we understand what baptism means then we can understand why infant baptism is important.

Holy Baptism is the basis of the whole Christian life, the gateway to life in the spirit and the door which gives access to the other sacraments. Through baptism we are freed from sin and reborn as sons of God; we become members of Christ, are incorporated into the Church, and made sharers in her mission:

> *"Baptism is the sacrament of regeneration through water in the word"* (CCC 1213).

Born with a fallen human nature and tainted by original sin, children also have need of the new birth in baptism to be freed from the power of darkness and brought into the realm of the freedom of the children of God, to which all men are called. The sheer gratuitousness of the grace of salvation is particularly manifest in infant baptism.

The Church and the parents would deny a child the priceless grace of becoming a child of God were they not to confer baptism shortly after birth (CCC 1250).

According to the Oration of St. Gregory Nazianzus, "*Baptism (which in practical term means Immersion — to be buried into Christ's death and to rise with Christ as a new creature) is God's most beautiful and magnificent gift... We call it gift, grace, anointing, enlightenment, garment of immortality, bath of rebirth, seal, and most precious gift. It is called gift because it is conferred on those who bring nothing of their own; grace since it is given even to the guilty; Baptism because sin is buried in the water; anointing for it is priestly and royal as are those who are anointed; enlightenment because it radiates light; clothing since it veils our shame; bath because it washes; and seal as it is our guard and the sign of God's Lordship.*"

Where is infant baptism in the bible?

Baptism holds a central place in the Christian faith, signifying the initiation into the Christian community and the purification from sin. While the practice of infant baptism has been questioned by some, it is deeply rooted in biblical teachings and holds profound theological significance.

The question, "where is it in the bible?", often causes fear and hesitation among many Catholics resulting in a sense of incapacity to openly express their faith and doctrinal beliefs. However, it is important to consider that although modern inventions are not explicitly mentioned in the Bible, we utilize them today for evangelization in accordance with the teachings of Christ, which instruct us:

> *"Go then, to all people everywhere and make them my disciples, baptize them in the name of the Father and of the Son and of the Holy Spirit"* (Matthew 28:19).

It is also important to note that Jesus did not place limitations on baptism. In fact, he showed displeasure when his disciples tried to prevent children from approaching him (Matthew 19:14). Just as circumcision was a sign of God's covenant with Abraham and his descendants in the Old Testament, infant baptism signifies the continuity of God's covenant in the New Testament. In Joshua 24:15, Joshua declares, *"As for me and my household, we will serve the Lord."* This commitment to serve the Lord as a household aligns with the Catholic belief in baptizing infants as part of a family's faith journey.

In Acts 16:14-15, the story of Lydia portrays a significant aspect of infant baptism. Lydia, a seller of purple cloth, was a worshipper of God. After hearing the message of Paul, she and her entire household were baptized. This account suggests that Lydia's entire household, which likely included children, received baptism as an expression of their faith.

The Catholic Church believes in the salvific nature of baptism, which cleanses individuals from sin and grants them forgiveness. In Acts 2:38, Peter urges the people to repent and be baptized for the forgiveness of their sins. This understanding extends to infants as well, as they, too, are born with original sin and can benefit from the grace of baptism.

Jesus emphasized the importance of being born again in order to enter the Kingdom of God. In John 3:5, Jesus tells Nicodemus, "*Truly, truly, I say to you, unless one is born of water and the Spirit, he cannot enter the kingdom of God.*" This teaching underscores the transformative power of baptism, where individuals, including infants, are born anew through the sacrament.

Throughout the New Testament, there are instances of entire households being baptized, implying the inclusion of children. In Acts 16:33, after the jailer's conversion, Paul and Silas baptized him and "all his family." This practice aligns with the Catholic understanding that baptism is a sacrament for the entire household, including infants, reflecting God's inclusive love.

Infant baptism in the Catholic tradition finds its biblical foundation in the continuity of God's covenant, as exemplified by Joshua's declaration. It is supported by the conversion of Lydia and her household, emphasizing the inclusion of children in the sacrament. The teachings on baptism for the forgiveness of sins and new birth, as expressed by Jesus, provide further validation. Moreover, the instances of household baptisms throughout the New Testament reinforce the understanding that infants can receive this sacrament. In embracing infant baptism, the Catholic Church acknowledges the importance of initiating children into the faith community, nurturing their spiritual growth, and providing them with the grace of God from an early age.

HOLY EUCHARIST

What is the Holy Eucharist, and Can a Non-catholic Christian Receive the Holy Eucharist?

Rev. Fr. Ugochukwu Ugwoke (ISch)

The Eucharist is one of the seven sacraments of the Catholic Church. According to the Catechism of the Catholic Church, the Holy Eucharist is the sacrament of the Body and Blood of Jesus Christ (CCC 1328-1331). The Holy Eucharist is also called Holy Communion because:

> *"by this sacrament, we unite ourselves to Christ, who makes us sharers in his Body and Blood to form a single body"* (CCC 1331).

The Eucharist was instituted by Jesus Christ during his last supper with his disciples before his death (Matthew 26:17-29; Mark 14:12-25; Luke 22:7-38).

The Catholic Church is open to people from all faith and culture. For instance, anyone irrespective of faith can take part in the celebration of the Holy Mass in which the Eucharist is offered and received. However, not everyone including Catholics themselves who take part in a Mass can receive the Holy Eucharist. The Holy Eucharist or Communion is properly the sacrament of those who are 'in full communion' with the Church (CCC 1395). The Catholic Church only allows those who are her members, that is, those either baptized into the Catholic faith (baptism is the gateway to other sacraments) or those who have been received into the Church through the profession of faith to receive the Eucharist. If the Church allowed those who are not united with or in the Church to receive Eucharist, she would seem to be asserting that those who are not in communion with the Church may take part in the very sacrament which definitively marks such communion (1 Corinthians 11:27-29).

Unlike other Christian churches, the Catholic Church believes that the Eucharist is the true Body and Blood of Jesus Christ (Matthew 26:26-28, John 6:41-56). The Eucharist for us Catholics is not merely symbolic; Jesus is truly present in the Eucharist. As such, another reason we cannot share the Eucharist with other Christians is because they do not share the same belief with us about the Eucharist. The one exception which the Code of the Canon Law makes is that in the danger of death or in the face of other grave necessity, in the judgment of the diocesan bishop orthe conference of bishops, Catholic ministers may illicitly administer the sacrament of Eucharist to other baptized non-Catholic Christians who do not have full Communion with the Catholic Church, who cannot approach a minister of their own faith community and on their own ask for it, provided they manifest Catholic faith in this sacrament and are properly disposed" (Code of Canon Law, 844 & 4, CCC 1401). These cases are exceptional, however often characterized by extreme or dire circumstances and each case must be treated singly.

In all, if a person is not Catholic and does not desire to be Catholic, then, they do not desire this communion with the Church. If a non-Catholic shares our faith about the Eucharist, the Church will gladly share Holy Communion with him or her. However, before receiving, such a person needs to enter the full communion of the Church established by Christ the Lord through formal instruction such as the Rites of Christian Initiation of Adults or other means of catechesis.

MASS

How is Mass a Prayer?

Rev. Fr. Maximilian Nwosu

St Therese of Lisieux wrote in her "Manuscripts" that prayer is a surge of the heart, a simple look towards heaven, a cry of recognition and love. And our simple catechism expresses prayer as the raising of one's mind and heart to God and that the desire for God is written in the human heart, because man is created by God and for God. God never ceases to draw man to himself and only in God will mankind find the truth and happiness. Thus, St Augustine writes: "*You are great, O Lord and greatly to be praised, You have made us for yourself, and our heart is restless until it rests in you.*" Man's desire for God drives him to a communion with God in the greatest prayer called "The Mass." In the old days, when all the prayers were in Latin, the last words said were *"Ite, missa est."* It meant, *"go, you are sent."* The word *"missa"* came to be used to describe the entire prayer!

The Second Vatican Council explains that the Holy Mass is the source and summit of our Christian life. The Mass (Eucharist meaning thanksgiving) is the greatest prayer we can offer since it is Christ's prayer, Christ's saving sacrifice offered to the heavenly Father for his glory and for our salvation. At every Mass, Christ unites us to himself in the offering of this prayer, of this sacrifice. A Sacrifice of atonement, adoration, thanksgiving, and supplication.

At the Holy Mass, Jesus Christ is the priest offering the sacrifice of Mass and at the same time the Lamb/oblation for the sacrifice. There is no other prayer where Jesus Christ offers the prayer himself except at the Holy Mass. The Constitution on the Sacred Liturgy offers a summary the Eucharist i.e. the Mass.

> *"At the Last Supper, on the night when He was betrayed, our Saviour instituted the eucharistic sacrifice of His Body and Blood. He did this in order to perpetuate the sacrifice of the Cross throughout the centuries until He should come again, and so to entrust to His beloved spouse, the Church, a memorial of His death and resurrection: a sacrament of love, a sign of unity, a bond of charity, a paschal banquet in which Christ is eaten, the mind is filled with grace, and a pledge of future glory is given to us"* (Sacrosanctum Concilium, No. 47; cf. CCC 1323).

The General Instruction of the Roman Missal (No. 93) identifies the role of the priest in that as he prays Holy Mass, he does so in the person of Christ, he presides over the faithful and proclaims the word of salvation, he associates the faithful with himself in the offering of Christ's sacrifice and he conducts the rites with humility. The priest leads the gathered people in this greatest Christian prayer.

A simple explanation of the structure of the Holy Mass helps for more understanding. The priest enters and reverences the altar of sacrifice. He greets the people with the words of the resurrected Christ when he met his disciples — *"Peace be with you."* The congregants are invited to seek pardon from God (*Kyrie – Lord have mercy*) and then glorify God (*Gloria*). They listen to God speak to them (*Bible readings*) and profess belief in God (*Credo — I believe*). They make supplications (*Prayer of the faithful*) and offer gifts for the sacrifice (*Presentation of offertory gifts*). They give thanks and adore God (*Eucharistic prayers*), commune with God at the reception of the Holy Communion and are sent into the world by Christ to spread the Gospel *(Ite missa est).*

CONFIRMATION

What is the Difference Between the Anointing at Baptism and Confirmation?

Rev. Fr. Boniface Nkem Anusiem (PhD)

The first shot at this question would be to understand or refresh our understanding of the nature and character of the sacraments of Baptism and Confirmation. We must note first that they form the sacraments of Christian initiation together with the Holy Eucharist. According to the Code of the Canon Law (842:1), they are interrelated and indispensable for full integration into the life of the Church.

The Catechism of the Catholic Church (1213) gives the following details about the sacrament of Baptism:

Holy Baptism

Holy Baptism is the basis of the whole Christian life, the gateway to life in the Spirit (*vitae spiritualis ianua*), and the door which gives access to the other sacraments. Through Baptism, we are freed from sin and reborn as sons of God; we become members of Christ, are incorporated into the Church, and made sharers in her mission: "*Baptism is the sacrament of regeneration through water in the word.*"

The sacrament of Baptism opens the door to the Christian life. In other words, the first step toward becoming a Christian is receiving the sacrament of Baptism. Our Lord Jesus Christ demonstrated the importance of the sacrament by receiving the Baptism of John (Matthew 3:13-17). He also made it part of the evangelization tool for his disciples when commissioning them to make disciples of all nations (Matthew 28:19).

Sacrament of Confirmation

On the other hand, Confirmation functions in conferring the Holy Spirit on the recipients in a peculiar way to the end that they become fervent in the profession of their faith as perfect Christians and soldiers of Jesus Christ.

There are some scriptural foundations of the sacrament of Confirmation. In the Old Testament, the Prophet Joel (Joel 2:28-29) talks about God pouring His Spirit upon all flesh in the latter days.

Our Lord Jesus Christ received the Holy Spirit at his baptism in the Jordan (Matthew 3:16) and promised to send another Advocate from the Father to be with his disciples forever (John 14:16).

The most significant scriptural reference to the sacrament of Confirmation was the outpouring of the Holy Spirit on the apostles and others on the day of Pentecost as was promised by our Lord Jesus Christ shortly before His ascension into heaven (Acts 1:4-5; 8).

The difference between the sacraments of Baptism and Confirmation is a very subtle one in the strict sense because they share a common ground as the Holy Spirit is received;

in fact, the Catechism of the Catholic Church (1285) recommends that:

> *It must be explained to the faithful that the reception of the sacrament of Confirmation is necessary for the completion of baptismal grace. For by the sacrament of Confirmation [the baptized] are more perfectly bound to the Church and are enriched with a special strength of the Holy Spirit.*

Baptism can be received by an unbaptized person, infant, or adult. But Confirmation is strictly administered to baptized adults or Catechumens who could receive the three sacraments of initiation same time, especially on the Easter Vigil.

In the administration of the two sacraments, there are striking differences in terms of matter (materials used) and form (the words used). The table below gives us some clarity.

Sacrament	Matter	Form
Baptism	Water poured/ immersed three times.	N. I baptize you in the name of the Father, Son, and the Holy Spirit

PENANCE

Why Do Catholics Confess to Their Priests?

Rev. Fr. Paschal Okpaleke (PhD)

The practice of sacramental confession among Catholics is grounded in the Scriptures. In the post-resurrection appearance, Jesus said to his disciples:

> *"Receive the Holy Spirit. If you forgive the sins of any, they are forgiven; if you retain the sins of any, they are retained"* (John 20:22-23).

This instruction becomes a part of the Apostolic Creed that Catholics profess: *'I believe in ... the forgiveness of sins.'* According to the Catechism of the Catholic Church faith in the forgiveness is associated

> *"not only with faith in the Holy Spirit, but also with faith in the Church and in the communion of saints"* (CCC 976)

because the forgiveness of sins happens through the power of the Holy Spirit and even the faithful departed can benefit from this power.

The Catechism goes further to state that through the sacrament of Penance (which is another expression for sacramental Confession),

> *"the baptized can be reconciled with God and with the Church"* (CCC 980).

This point has been made in the Council of Trent that this sacrament is important for salvation because it constantly restores us to the status of being cleansed of sin that we experience at baptism. It renews our baptismal innocence each time and offers us the opportunity to access the unconditional love of God and the overflow of the grace of divine forgiveness.

But why confess to the priest, still?

First, the Gospel of John cited above shows that the power to absolve sins was specifically given to the apostles and not to everyone in the community. It is a power that is exercised by the priests because of its sacramental nature. This does not preclude the injunction to forgive one another as we recite in Our Lord's Prayer (Matthew6:12, 14-15).

Second, the Catholic understanding of sacrament presents to us the profound relationship between God and humanity. In this relationship, the Church is identified as a sign and instrument of humanity's communion with God and of unity among believers (*Lumen Gentium* no.1). In that sense, the priest represents the Church in the reconciliation (and so, the maintenance of communion) between God and humanity that takes place during confession. This explains why during absolution, he prays *"through the ministry of the Church, may God grant you pardon and peace...."* This is part of the reason confession is also called the Sacrament of Reconciliation.

Third, following the above reasons, the priest does not act on his own accord. He is only but a servant and minister of this sacrament and not the "*master of God's forgiveness*" (CCC 1466). As such the person who confesses his or her sins addresses God and not the priest. This is shown especially at the beginning where he or she says, "*Forgive me Father for I have sinned.*" The 'Father' refers to God, who alone has the power to forgive sins. Another point is the Act of Contrition, where the penitent prays:

"O my God, I am heartily sorry for having offended Thee, and I detest all my sins because of thy just punishments, but most of all because they offend Thee, my God, who art all good and deserving of all my love. I firmly resolve with the help of Thy grace to sin no more and to avoid the near occasion of sin. Amen."

Indeed, a penitent does not need to be afraid of opening up to the priest at the confessional. In consideration of our human instinct of self-preservation, most confessionals are constructed in a way that safeguards the anonymity of the penitent. Meanwhile, a priest is bound to keep the confessional seal (CCC 1467) even under the pain of death. Any priest that breaks the confessional seal faces automatic (latae sententiae) excommunication (Canon 1388 §1). This is one of the most critical aspects of priestly training and the most beautiful dimension of this sacrament: that the priest is ready to be punished or even to die rather than reveal the sins we confessed privately.

PENANCE

Can Confession Be Done Online or Through Third-party Means?

Rev. Fr. Paschal Okpaleke (PhD)

This question becomes pertinent in this contemporary age where a lot is happening online, including religious practices, heightened by the COVID pandemic. The online participation at Mass has raised the question of the sacramentality of the Eucharistic celebration, with many theologians and pastors dismissing it as unsustainable. As such, it can only be a temporary choice in a case where it is impracticable to attend Mass physically. Apart from the Eucharistic, the question is also posed when it comes to sacramental confession.

It is good to recall that the Catechism teaches that sacramental confession is "a liturgical action." As every liturgy, it is embodied in all its elements

> *"a greeting and blessing from the priest, reading the word of God to illuminate the conscience and elicit contrition, and an exhortation to repentance; the confession, which acknowledges sins and makes them known to the priest; the imposition and acceptance of a penance; the priest's absolution; a prayer of thanksgiving and praise and dismissal with the blessing of the priest"* (CCC 1480).

Thus, it is quite difficult to effectively exercise this action online without our bodily participation.

In most cases, the confession is integrated within a larger communal liturgical celebration that prepares the faithful for the sacrament. This ceremony might include elements such as examination of conscience, liturgy of the Word, the Lord's Prayer, and common thanksgiving. Such a

> *"communal celebration expresses more clearly the ecclesial character of penance"* (CCC 1482).

Notwithstanding the option of general absolution of sins, the individual confession is at once a liturgical, communal, and public act of the Church. Additionally, the secrecy and privacy of personal confession could easily be violated when conducted online. Since sacraments are at the heart of our Catholic faith, the Church is always careful in avoiding anything that would trivialize these instruments of God's redeeming quality in our lives. Of course, there are attempts to develop digital apps that could guarantee the secrecy of online confession. But to what extent can we trust technology? Besides, since confession is between the penitent and God with the priest doing a representative function, any introduction of a third element puts at grave risk the privacy, secrecy, and personal character of the sacrament.

On the question of whether one can confess through a third party, the general answer is that this is not allowed given the personal character of confession. However, the canon law foresees that it is possible to confess using an interpreter, but there is no obligation on the part of the penitent to do so. This is especially in cases of grave "physical or moral impossibility," for instance in cases of grave speech impediment or illness or lack of common language between the confessor and the penitent. In that case, the interpreter is equally bound to keep the confessional seal (Canon 983 § 2). In Canon 990, we read:

> *"No one is prohibited from confessing through an interpreter as long as abuses and scandals are avoided and without prejudice to the prescript of" (Canon 983 § 2).*

PENANCE

What is the Difference Between Mortal Sin and Venial Sin?

Rev. Fr. Boniface Nkem Anusiem (PhD)

Sin results from a wrong choice made in defiance of divine precepts. The New Testament Greek rendering of ′sin is αμαρτία (hamartia) which means missing the mark as drawn from the game of archery. So, to sin means missing a set mark or falling short of an expectation.

The first recorded sin on earth was the disobedience of Adam and Eve (Genesis 3:11). So, we define sin as the transgression of God's laws or commandments (1 John 3:4). The Catechism of the Catholic Church (1849) says:

> *Sin is an offense against reason, truth, and right conscience; it is failure in genuine love for God and neighbour caused by a perverse attachment to certain goods. It wounds the nature of man and injures human solidarity. It has been defined as "an utterance, a deed, or a desire contrary to the eternal law."*

The distinction between "mortal" and "venial" sin comes from the First Letter of John (1 John 5:17), which says, *"All wrongdoing is sin, but there is sin that is not mortal."* Expanding on the two dimensions of sin, the Catechism of the Catholic Church teaches that sin is mortal when the object is a "*grave matter, committed with full knowledge and deliberate consent*" (CCC 1857). The Ten Commandments (Exodus 20:1-17) give us a perfect example of mortal sin.

Sin is venial when the three preconditions of mortal sin are not in the equation. That means the gravity of the matter is less, and full knowledge and consent are lacking. Describing sin as venial does not mean that it could be neglected because venial sin could graduate to mortal sin when unchecked. The Catechism of the Catholic Church (1863) teaches:

> *Venial sin weakens charity; it manifests a disordered affection for created goods; it impedes the soul's progress in the exercise of the virtues and the practice of the moral good; it merits temporal punishment deliberate and unrepented venial sin disposes us little by little to commit mortal sin.*

Sin generally attacks the grace of God in us, and that is why the church requires being in "the state of grace" to be able to receive the Holy Eucharist. The state of grace is when we are completely in alignment with God. Mortal sin pushes us away completely from God, while venial sin pushes us to the margins of the divine ambiance. Consider the following diagram for more pictorial clarification.

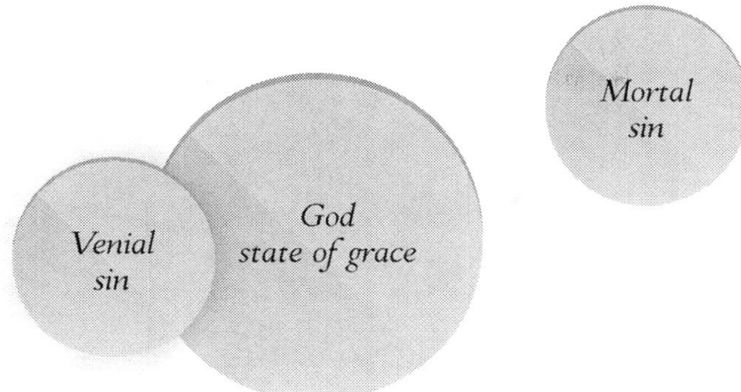

We conclude our brief interface of the distinction between mortal and venial sin by reminding ourselves about the need to make frequent visits to the sacrament of penance. Regular and effective confession helps to keep ourselves in check with the evasion of sin in our lives. John's First Letter (1 John 2:1-2) says:

> *"My little children, I am writing this to you so that you may not sin; but if anyone does sin, we have an advocate with the Father, Jesus Christ the righteous; and he is the expiation for our sins, and not for ours only but also for the sins of the entire world."*

Unfortunately, most Catholics in our day and age are losing the traditional sense of sin and the obligation to confess our sins; in fact, the sacrament of penance could also be regarded as the "forgotten sacrament." Starting from you, when was the last time you had a productive confession of your sins in true repentance?

PENANCE

What is Indulgence and How Can One Receive It?

Rev. Fr. Paschal Okpaleke (PhD)

It must be noted that indulgence is intricately linked to the sacrament of reconciliation. The Canon Law offers a noticeably clear definition of indulgence:

> *"An indulgence is a remission before God of the temporal punishment due to sins whose guilt has already been forgiven, which the faithful Christian who is duly disposed gains under certain prescribed conditions through the action of the Church which, as the minister of redemption, dispenses and applies with authority the treasury of the satisfactions of Christ and the saints"* (Canon 992).

To simplify this, we must note that there is a double consequence to every sin. The Catechism explains:

> *"Grave sin deprives us of communion with God and therefore makes us incapable of eternal life.... On the other hand, every sin, even venial, entails an unhealthy attachment to creatures, which must be purified either here on earth, or after death in the state called Purgatory.*

This purification frees one from what is called the 'temporal punishment' of sin" (CCC 1472).

These two consequences are not inflicted by God but flow from the very nature of sin. However, we can attain complete purification of our sins without these consequent punishments if our conversion proceeds from a place of true charity. This can happen through prayer, penance, works of mercy and charity until we completely dispose our sinful selves and become new creatures in Christ. The Church can offer indulgences based on the power to bind and to unbind that was given to it by Christ. Nevertheless, the intention of the Church is not just to offer a miraculous act that dispels all punishments due to sin, but to motivate the faithful to *"works of devotion, penance, and charity"* (CCC 1478). For instance, a single sacramental confession that one makes can obtain several plenary indulgences.

Meanwhile, we must note that there are two types of indulgence, namely partial or plenary, which removes respectively either *"part or all of the temporal punishment due to sin"* (Canon 993). Both forms of indulgence can be gained either for oneself or can be applied to the dead (Canon 994), as this is consistent with the Catholic faith in the communion of saints. A plenary indulgence applicable to the dead can be obtained on November 2, the feast of All Souls. The Catechism while referencing Pope Paul VI's 1967 apostolic constitution, Indulgentiarum Doctrina (no.5), remarks that under the doctrine of the communion of saints, *"a perennial link of charity exists between the faithful who have already reached their heavenly home, those who are expiating their sins in purgatory and those who are still pilgrims on earth. Between them there is, too, an abundant exchange of all good things."* Thus, within this noble communion,

> *"the holiness of one profits others well beyond the harm that the sin of one could cause others. Thus, recourse to the communion of saints lets the contrite sinner be more promptly and efficaciously purified of the punishments for sin" (CCC 1475).*

Any baptized person who seeks plenary indulgence must have the intention of gaining it and must fulfil the prescribed works accordingly (Canon 996 § 2), including the three conditions of: sacramental confession, Eucharistic Communion, and prayer for the intention of the Pope, which may be satisfied by reciting one 'Our Father' and one 'Hail Mary' or any other prayer freely chosen by the faithful (Indulgentiarum Doctrina no.12, n.7, n.10). He or she must not be under excommunication, and in the state of grace *"at least at the end of the prescribed works"* (Canon 996 & 1). Meanwhile, a devout visit to a church or oratory and the recitation of an 'Our Father' and the 'Creed' are the acts needed in obtaining plenary indulgences that are connected with a church or oratory (Indulgentiarum Doctrina, no.12, n.16). As for partial indulgence, one can get that through the devout use of *"an object of piety (crucifix, cross, rosary, scapular, or medal) properly blessed by any priest"* (n.17).

EXTREME-UNCTION

What Happens if a Catholic Dies Without the Sacrament of Extreme Unction/anointing of the Sick?

Rev. Fr. Johnpromise Umeozuru

According to St Thomas Aquinas, *"...a sacrament properly so called is that which is the sign of some sacred thing pertaining to man; sign of a holy thing so far as it makes men holy."* It is from this definition of a sacrament that the Church teaches that:

> *"The sacraments are efficacious signs of grace, instituted by Christ and entrusted to the Church, by which divine life is dispensed to us."*

It is a truism that the seven sacraments were instituted by Christ and are necessary for salvation for all believers.

Healing of the sick has been part of our salvific history since it is through disobedience that suffering, sickness and death entered the world (Genesis 3:16-19). We see this in the healing of Tobit's blindness in Tobit 11:15, and in Wisdom 16:12. In the New Testament, Christ became the healer of all diseases and infirmities as we read in Mark 7:32-36, and in sending out the Twelve to anoint and heal the sick in Mark 6:13. It was based on the above mandate that St James encouraged Christians to send for the elders of the Church to anoint them with oil and pray over them for healing when they are sick. During the Middle Ages and with the reforms by Charles the Great, three sacraments of Penance, Extreme Unction and Viaticum became known as the last rites of the Church to be administered by priests when someone is about to die. Regarding the issue at hand, the Church teaches:

> *"God has bound salvation to the sacrament of Baptism, but he himself is not bound by his sacraments."*

Although the sacraments are essential for salvation, and the Church is necessary for salvation, they are not the only means our salvation is guaranteed. However, anyone who knowingly rejects the Church and her sacraments, rejects God and His grace, and cannot be saved.

Hence, any Catholic who has lived his/her life in keeping with Matthew 25:31-46, observed a good and prayerful

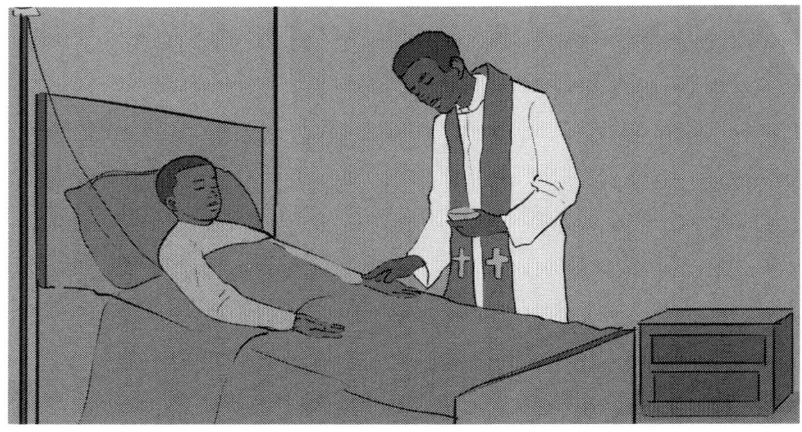

life, availed himself/herself of the sacraments, when possible, should not fear death. However, the Sacrament of Anointing of the Sick confers a "special grace" to the person preparing for the journey heavenward.

HOLY ORDERS

Ministerial Priesthood Versus Ordinary Priesthood

Rev. Fr. Kelvin Ugwu (MSP)

I flipped through the pages of my bible, an old crispy gift I got from my late dad many years ago. I perused the pages and my eyes caught the precious letter written by St Peter. I read a part of it, the place that caught my eye, and a particular verse was staring at me, and started living rent-free in my head. It says:

> *"You, however, are a chosen race, a royal priesthood, a holy nation, a purchased people"* (1 Peter 2:9).

Of all the qualities and definitions from St Peter concerning all of us who are the body of Christ, the use of the phrase "A Royal Priesthood" is indeed deep and worthy of further clarification because the phrase gives life to the fact that we all are consecrated as priests, not just priests, but royal priests.

The Royal Priesthood

The question is: what really does it mean when he referred to us as Royal Priesthood?

The use of this term is drawn from the Septuagint version of the bible, it is a direct quotation from Exodus 19:6. "*You will be for me a kingdom of priests and a holy nation.*" The phrase "*Kingdom of Priests*" would mean an organized empire, of which every member is a priest. The obvious question will be "Does it mean everyone is a priest in the same way Aaron is"? Also, "Why the Levite priest if everyone is a priest"?

The answer to the above question is rooted in the sacrament of Baptism. In its true essence, the sacramental character conferred on those who receive the sacrament of baptism is first and foremost the power to participate in the Paschal mystery, which is summarized in the dying and rising of Jesus in which the Eucharist is the centre.

The Catechism of the Catholic Church tells us that

> *"by Baptism, (the baptized) share in the priesthood of Christ, in his prophetic and royal mission" (CCC 1268).*

It is the baptism that in-cooperates everyone, giving all of us a single identity.

Through baptism, all the faithful share in the priesthood of Christ; this is what has been called the "*common priesthood of the faithful*". In addition to this priesthood and to serve it, there is another form of participation in Christ's mission: the ministry conferred with the Sacrament of Orders or the "*ministerial Priesthood*" (*CCC* 1591).

The common priesthood versus the ministerial priesthood

The liturgy is the action of the whole Mystical Body of Christ, Head, and members (*Sacrosanctum Concilium,* n. 7). It is the action of all the faithful because they all participate in the priesthood of Christ. However, all do not have the same function, because all do not participate in the same way in the priesthood of Christ.

However, the Magisterium documents in 1997 (*Ecclesiae de Mysterio, Instruction on Certain Questions regarding the Collaboration of the Non-Ordained Faithful in the Sacred Ministry of Priests,* Premiss), and most especially the document of the Second Vatican Council, present and clarify the principle of the different identities, the distinction between the "common priesthood" and the "ministerial priesthood", common dignity and mission, and the difference of functions of the laity, sacred ministers and religious.

The teaching of the Church is clear regarding the essential distinction between the two ways in which the Church participates in the one priesthood of Jesus. Both participations are ordered to one another and depend on one another yet are essentially different from one another.

> *"Though they differ from one another in essence and not only in degree, the common priesthood of the faithful and the ministerial or hierarchical priesthood are nonetheless interrelated: each of them in its own special way is a participation in the one priesthood of Christ"* (Letter of His Holiness John Paul II to Priests for Holy Thursday 1996).

The second Vatican document of the church (Lumen Gentium no.10) gives an explicit distinction between the "common priesthood" and the "ministerial priesthood".

The common priesthood

The common priesthood of believers refers to the belief that all baptized individuals share in the priestly ministry of Jesus Christ. This means that every member of the Church has a role in offering spiritual sacrifices and participating in the mission of spreading the Gospel.

Through baptism, all believers are united with Christ and become part of His priestly people. As priestly people then, they are called to offer their daily lives as a spiritual sacrifice, living in accordance with the teachings of Christ and actively participating in the worship and service of the Church.

The common priesthood of believers emphasizes the dignity and responsibility of every Christian. It recognizes that each person has a unique calling and gifts to contribute to the building up of the Church and the proclamation of the Good News.

In 1 Peter 2:9, it is written, *"But you are a chosen people, a royal priesthood, a holy nation, God's special possession, that you may declare the praises of him who called you out of darkness into his wonderful light."* This verse highlights the special status of believers as a royal priesthood.

Furthermore, Revelation 1:6 states, *"And made us a kingdom, priests to our God and Father; to him be glory and dominion forever and ever. Amen."* This verse affirms the priestly role of all believers, who are part of the kingdom of God.

The common priesthood of believers underscores the notion that the Church encompasses not only ordained ministers but also all the faithful. It emphasizes the significance of active participation, spiritual growth, and the collective responsibility of nurturing and strengthening the Body of Christ.

The ministerial priesthood

The ministerial priesthood, also known as the hierarchical priesthood, is rooted in the sacrament of Holy Orders. Through this sacrament, individuals receive a sacramental character that configures them to Christ, who is the Head and Spouse of the Church (Lumen Gentium, 28).

In the ministerial priesthood, Jesus is sacramentally present. It is through this sacramental presence that the risen Christ unites His sacrifice with the spiritual sacrifices of all the baptized in the celebration of the Eucharist. The ministerial priest, acting in the person of Jesus, allows Jesus, the Head and Spouse of the Church, to make the Church part of His self-offering in the Eucharist and to bestow His redemptive grace upon the Church through the sacraments (Lumen Gentium, 10).

The ministerial priesthood holds a crucial role in the life of the Church. Ordained ministers are called to serve the faithful by proclaiming the Word of God, administering the sacraments, and providing pastoral care. They are entrusted with the sacred responsibility of leading the community in worship, guiding the faithful on their spiritual journey, and offering guidance and counsel (Lumen Gentium, 28).

In the New Testament, Jesus institutes the ministerial priesthood when He appoints the apostles as His chosen ones, granting them the authority to forgive sins and celebrate the Eucharist (Matthew 16:19, Luke 22:19). St. Paul affirms the importance of the ministerial priesthood in his letter to the Corinthians, stating,

> *"This is how one should regard us, as servants of Christ and stewards of the mysteries of God"* (1 Corinthians 4:1).

It is important to note that the ministerial priesthood we refer to here is the priesthood of Christ according to the order of Melchizedek (Hebrews 5:6), different and superior to the Aaronic priesthood of the Old Testament. The priesthood of Christ represents a new covenant and a new way of approaching God, offering redemption, forgiveness, and eternal salvation to all who believe in Him. Through His priesthood, Christ opens the way for believers to have direct access to God and experience reconciliation with Him.

Finally, the ministerial priesthood serves as a vital instrument in the Church's mission to spread the Gospel and sanctify the faithful. Through their ordained ministry, these priests act as shepherds, guiding and nurturing the people of God, and serving as a visible sign of Christ's presence among His followers.

MARRIAGE

Can a Catholic Marry a Non-catholic Partner in the Catholic Church?

Friar Paul Orerhime Akpomie (OP)

The Catholic Church does not prohibit Catholics from marrying people who are not Catholics. There are two types of these marriages. On one hand, we have "mixed marriages." A mixed marriage is one between Catholics and Christians who are not Catholic persons. On the other hand, we have "marriages of disparity of cults." Such marriages are those between Catholics and persons who are not Christians; for instance, Muslims, atheists, adherents of African Traditional Religions (ATR), and other forms of spiritualism. In both marriage cases, it is important to note that oneof the purposes of the Church's existence is to safeguard the souls of her children. All sacraments are set up by Jesus Christ for sanctification of souls.

Marriage is one of the seven sacraments of the Church. The celebration of the rites of sacraments makes Christ present in our midst for the good of the individuals, or the couple, and for the community. Marriage between two baptized catholics is a sacramental marriage. If a Catholic insists on a mixed marriage, or marriage of disparity of cult, both types of marriages can be validly entered into but are non-sacramental marriages. While the Catholic Church allows it, she still conducts her role as mother of the faithful to protect the soul of the Catholic in the marriage by making sure the non-Catholic understands the moral teaching and obligations of the Catholic party and assure that the Catholic is not in a position hostile to his or her faith.

For validity of marriage, the Catholic Church holds that four elements must be present: First, the spouses are free and not coerced to marry. Second, consent of marital vows is freely exchanged. Third, the right intention of marriage to marry for life, to be faithful to one another, and be open to children, must be present. Fourth, the consent of the couple is given before two witnesses and in the presence of an authorized Church minister.

For both forms of marriages, that is, marriage between the Catholic and baptized Christian of different denominations; and the marriage between a Catholic and non-Christian, permission from the local Bishop to marry is needed. The permission is called a "permission to enter into mixed marriage," if the person is non-Catholic Christian. If the person is not a Christian, the permission is called a "dispensation from disparity of cult." In cases where the future spouse, either non-Catholic Christian, or non-Christian, chooses to become Catholic before marrying a Catholic, the program called the Rite of Adult Christian Initiation (RCIA) is followed by the individual.

It is not necessary to become Catholic, but the Catholic must uphold the obligation to preserve his or her own faith and

> *"ensure the baptism and education of the children in the Catholic Church."* (CCC 1635).

Baptized Catholics in marriages are channels for conveying grace to others. Scripture tells us that the unbelieving spouse is made holy through the believing spouse (1 Corinthians 7:14). In a mixed-marriage, or disparity of cult the Catholic is a conduit of grace to the non-believer. If this leads to a free conversion of belief by the non-believer, then the Church rejoices.

MARRIAGE

Why is Divorce Not Accepted in the Church?

Friar Paul Orerhime Akpomie (OP)

The Catholic Church's teaching on divorce is built on Jesus Christ teaching about marriage and divorce. In Matthew 19: 3-10, Jesus Christ responded to those who inquired about the lawfulness of divorce for any cause. He answered,

> *"Have you not read that he who made them from the beginning made them male and female, and said, 'For this reason a man shall leave his father and mother and be joined to his wife, and the two shall become one flesh'? So, they are no longer two but one flesh. What therefore God has joined together, let not man put asunder."*

They said to him,

> *"Why then did Moses command one to give a certificate of divorce, and to put her away?" He said to them, 'For your hardness of heart Moses allowed you to divorce your wives, but from the beginning it was not so. And I say to you: whoever divorces his wife, except for*

> *unchastity, and marries another, commits adultery.'"*

Evidently, Jesus sets up that marriage is a union between a male and a female, and that this is the will of the author of marriage, God, our heavenly Father. Marriage brings about an eternal and exclusive bond between the man and the woman, such that they couple are no longer two, but one flesh. This sacramental bond is not breakable, and it negates the act of divorce. Some individuals argue that there is an exception clause with regards to divorce. The phrase, *"except on the ground of unchastity,"* constitutes reason for divorce and remarriage in situations where one, or both spouses commit adultery. Such interpretations are caused by faulty reading of the text.

The word used for *"unchastity"* is the Greek word, *"porneia,"* which refers to unlawful sexual relationship between cohabiting individuals who are not validly married, though they live as if they were (cf. John 4:17-18). Concerning such situations, to separate and validly get married to another person does not constitute adultery. The reason for this is because the couple were not married in the first place. A valid marriage, however, cannot be dissolved. Christ said,

> *"They are no longer two but one flesh. What therefore God has joined together, let not man put asunder."*

There is noteworthy difference between a married person who has truly endeavoured to be faithful to the sacrament of marriage and is unjustly abandoned or divorced decreed by civil law; and one who through his own grave fault destroys a canonically valid marriage. The former has not contravened the moral law, whereas, the latter is guilty. (CCC 2386).

Divorce and remarriage are serious sins in God's law. We are warned that the unrighteous will not inherit the Kingdom of God. Adultery is listed as one of the sins of the unrighteous in 1 Corinthians 6:9- 10. For Catholics who find themselves in this quagmire, kindly go for sacramental confession and meet with your priest to help with advice and accompaniment to set things right.

Read further: Malachi 2:16, Matthew 5:31-32; 19:16-19, Romans 7:2-3.

SALVATION

Is There Salvation Apart From Christ?

Friar JudeMary Owoh (OP)

The Catholic Church teaches that, *"extra ecclesiam nulla salus,"*, translated as *"outside the Church there is no salvation."* This has its basis in the words of Christ,

> *"Truly I tell you; no one can see the kingdom of God unless they are born again"* (John 3:3).

But as with all teachings of the Faith, this has to be qualified and understood properly. The Catechism of the Catholic Church lays out the truth of the matter succinctly in paragraphs 830 and 846-848:

1. There is no salvation apart from Christ and his One, Holy, Catholic, and Apostolic Church.
2. Those who are ignorant (through no fault of theirs) concerning the truth of 1st above will not be culpable for this lack of knowledge before God.
3. Those in the category of 2 have the real possibility of salvation even if they never come to an explicit knowledge of Christ and/or his Church.

Not that simply because a person is "ignorant" of the truth, they will automatically be saved. Ignorance is not bliss; it is dangerous.

The Catechism of the Catholic Church, paragraphs 846-48 states:

> *"Basing itself on Scripture and Tradition, the- Council teaches that the Church, a pilgrim now on earth, is necessary for salvation: the one Christ is the mediator and the way of salvation; he is present to us in his body which is the Church. He himself explicitly asserted the necessity of faith and Baptism, and thereby affirmed at the same time the necessity of the Church which men enter through Baptism as through a door. Hence, they could not be saved who, knowing that the Catholic Church was founded as necessary by God through Christ, would refuse either to enter it or to remain in it".*

However, the Catechism continues:

> *"Although in ways known to himself God can lead those, who, through no fault of their own, are ignorant of the Gospel, to that faith without which it is impossible to please him, the Church still has the obligation and also the sacred right to evangelize all men" (quoting Ad Gentes, 7, a document from Vatican II).*

In John 14:6, Jesus said,

> *"I am the Way, the Truth and the Life, no man can come to the Father except by me."*

Christ is essential for salvation, and we are saved through the Church. He says,

> *"He who hears you hears me, and he who rejects you rejects me"* (Luke 10:16).

The Church is "*the fullness of him who fills all in all*" (Ephesians 1:23). The Church is Christ in the world. It is Almighty God who willed "*that through the church the manifold wisdom of God might now be made known*" (Ephesians 3:10). To reject the Church is to reject Christ because it was Christ who gave authority to the Church.

The bottom line is: the straight and narrow road that leads to heaven is not an easy road to begin with (see Matthew 7:13; 1 Peter 4:18). But without the Church and sacraments Christ has provided as the ordinary means for our sanctification, it is even more difficult.

PURGATORY

Why Do Catholics Believe in Purgatory?

Rev. Fr. Johnpromise Umeozuru

According to Joseph Cardinal Ratzinger, the doctrine of Purgatory is part of the dogmatic teaching of the Church on Eschatology. To understand this doctrine, we need to have a profound and comprehensive grasp of the theology of sin and its purification.

The word sin is derived from the Greek word *harmatia* which means: *'Missing the mark.'* This Greek word *"harmatia"* appears 174 times in the Greek text of the New Testament and refers to any deviation from perfect righteousness.

According to the Catechism:

> *"Sin is before all else an offence against God, a rupture of communion with God. At the same time, it damages communion with the Church."*

Since there are double consequences for sin – Eternal and Temporal Punishments; while the eternal punishment for sin "Eternal Damnation" is remitted through the Sacrament of Reconciliation, the temporal punishment of sin remains. This temporal punishment due to sin is satisfied by bearing all kinds of sufferings patiently and serenely here on earth, or after death in Purgatory.

In describing Purgatory, the Church states,

> *"All who die in God's grace and friendship, but still imperfectly purified, are indeed assured of their eternal salvation; but after death they undergo purification, so as to achieve the holiness necessary to enter the joy of heaven."*

This doctrinal teaching on Purgatory was formulated by the Church at the Councils of Florence and Trent while treating the issue of Indulgences.

The first biblical foundation in support of the above doctrine is the heroic act of Judas in 2nd Maccabees 12:32-45, when he collected money and sent it off to Jerusalem for a sin offering for those who were struck in battle because they had charms on them. He did this to make atonement for the dead to be delivered from sin.

The second one is 1 Corinthians 3:10-15 where St Paul made it clear that there is fire that guarantees salvation after some loss. According to him, any builder that does not build on the foundation that is Jesus Christ, will suffer loss, "*...will be saved, but only as through fire.*"

The Fathers of the Church like Tertullian in the West, Clement of Alexandria in the East and several saints upheld this teaching before it was officially formulated by the Church. Joseph Ratzinger gave us a succinct summary of Purgatory thus:

> *"Purgatory is the inwardly necessary process of transformation in which a person becomes capable of Christ, capable of God and thus capable of unity with the whole communion of saints".*

SAINTS

Why Do Catholics Pray for the Dead and to the Dead (Saints)?

Rev. Fr. Emmanuel Omokugbo Ojeifo (PhD)

In many religious cultures, death is recognized not as the end of life but as a rite of passage that prepares the spirit of the deceased to journey on to the next realm. Death facilitates the continuation of life in a new phase. In death a connection continues between the spirit of the dead person and their community on earth. Indeed, most world religions embody this understanding of death as establishing a relationship between the dead and the living.

In the Catholic Church, we speak of "the communion of saints" when we recite the Apostles' Creed. This communion is about a union, a common bond, a profound connection, a great fellowship. The communion has three states or ivisions: the communion of saints of the living, those who are still on their pilgrim journey on earth; and the communion of saints of the dead or the faithful departed, some of whom are being purified, those in purgatory, and the ones who are enjoying eternal glory in the presence ofGod, those in heaven (CCC 954).

In the Catholic Mass for the dead, the community through the Eucharistic preface makes this affirmation of faith when it prays: "*For your faithful, Lord, life is changed, not ended.*"

This means that death is not the end of life, but the change of life, from a transient existence in this world to an everlasting life with God and the saints in heaven. But as we already stated, some of the dead might still need purification from their sins before they can enjoy the presence of God. The basis of this belief is Revelation 21:27 which speaks of the Heavenly Jerusalem in these terms: "*But nothing that is impure will enter the city, nor anyone who does shameful things or tells lies. Only those whose names are written in the Lamb's book of the living will enter the city.*"

So why do Catholics pray for the dead? Because we are all frail, weak, and sinful human creatures, we can displease and offend God. By praying for the dead, the Church beseeches the Merciful God to be merciful in judging the dead person so that he/she may gain admittance into the heavenly company. We have affirmation from the mouth of Jesus that there is a possibility of obtaining forgiveness of sins in this age and in the age to come (Matthew 12:32). So, there is forgiveness of sins beyond death. The clearest affirmation of this in the Hebrew Scriptures is in Maccabees 12:38-45.

About the saints, these are those who "*have washed their robes white again in the blood of the Lamb. "That is why they stand before God's throne and serve him day and night in his temple*" (Revelation 7:14-17). They have great concern for us because they have communion with us. Because they are in God's presence, they can plead our cause, just as our guardian angels do (Matthew 18:10).

MARY

How is Mary the Mother of God?

Rev. Fr. Emmanuel Bekomson

There are still quite several Christians who, despite accepting the divinity of Jesus Christ, reject the idea that Mary is the Mother of God. The teaching of the Church on the Divine Motherhood of the Blessed Virgin Mary is quite clear and straightforward: Mary is the Mother of God because she is the Mother of Jesus Christ who Himself is God – the *Logos*, Second Person of the Blessed Trinity.

Sacred Scripture unreservedly presents Mary as the Mother of Jesus Christ. In the **Old Testament**, Isaiah foretells of a Virgin who shall "*conceive and bear a son and his name shall be called Emmanuel*" (Isaiah 7:14). In the **New Testament**, in Matthew, the birth of Jesus is presented as a fulfilment of this "Emmanuel" passage of Isaiah (Matthew 1:23). Mary is called "His (Jesus') mother" (Matthew 1:18; 2:11, 13, 20; 12:46; 13:55). This title is also used in John (John1:25-26; 2:1,3,5,12). In Luke however, what we find is a more elaborate presentation of the divine motherhood of Mary.

In the Annunciation narrative (Luke 1:26-45), she is heavily alluded to by the Angel as one who would give birth to the Son of the Most High (Luke 1:32, 35) and shall name him "Jesus" (Luke 1:31). Elizabeth, filled with the Holy

Spirit calls her "*Mother of my Lord*" (Luke 1:43). In the original Greek version of this text, *Kurios,* a term which has divine connotations is used to designate "Lord." The only reference to Mary in Pauline writings is in Galatians 4:4: "*God sent His Son, born of a woman...*" a further testimony to her being the Mother of the divine person, Jesus Christ.

The Divinity of Jesus is also rooted in Scripture, at the Baptism at Jordan, a voice from Heaven referred to him saying, "*This is my beloved Son in whom I am well pleased*" (Matthew 3:17; Mark 1:11; Luke 3:22; John 1:34), an expression that is also repeated at the Transfiguration (Matthew 17:5; Mark 9:7; Luke 9:35; 2Peter 1:17). This passage is a solemn revelation of the divine sonship of Jesus. Contrary to those who see this term merely as one of endearment, the expression "Son of God" is only used for Jesus in the New Testament. Jesus also reveals himself several times as the "*I am*" (John 4:26; 6:35, 41,48,51; 8:12, 23, 24, 28, 58; 9:5; 10:11, 30,36, 38; 11:25; 13:19; 14:6; 15:1; 18:5, 8). Scripture scholars often contrast the presentation of Jesus as the "*I am*" with the identification of God in the burning bush with the same title (Exodus 3:14), a further testimony to his divinity. It is this divine person, the Logos, who took flesh and dwelt among us (John 1:14), in the womb of the Blessed Virgin Mary.

The Council of Ephesus proclaimed in AD 431, that Mary truly became the mother of God by the human conception of the Son of God in her womb:

> *The Holy Fathers have not hesitated to speak of the holy Virgin as the Mother of God, not certainly because the nature of the Word or his divinity received the beginning of its ex-*

> *istence from the holy Virgin, but that, since the holy body, animated by a rational soul, which the Word of God united to himself according to the hypostasis, was born from her, the Word is said to be born according to the flesh.*

The Council Fathers therefore use the Greek term *Theotokos* (God-bearer or Mother of God) to describe her divine Motherhood, as opposed to the Nestorian *Anthropotokos* (Mother of Man) or *Christotokos* (Mother of Christ). Mary is therefore not just the mother of the human nature of Christ but the mother of the person of Jesus Christ, who himself is made up of a human and a divine nature.

Sadly, this view of the Nestorians is gaining popularity again in our day and is the backbone of the argument of those who reject the divine motherhood of Mary. The divine motherhood of the Blessed Virgin Mary is further re-echoed by the Fathers of the Second Vatican Council.

The Catechism of the Catholic Church expounds on this teaching in this way:

> *"...the One whom she conceived as man by the Holy Spirit, who truly became her Son according to the flesh, was none other than the Father's eternal Son, the Second Person of the Holy Trinity."*

One can see that the idea of the Divine Motherhood of the Blessed Virgin Mary, has its foundations in scripture and in the living Tradition of the Church, and so is not some idea concocted by some over-zealous and pious Catholics.

We can summarize our submissions with the affirmation that the Dogma of Mary's motherhood of God, as handed down by Sacred Scripture and Tradition contains two truths:

- *Mary is truly the Mother of Jesus.* She contributed everything to the formation of the human nature of Christ that every other mother contributes to the formation of their own child in their womb.
- *Mary is truly the Mother of God.* She conceived and bore, in the flesh, the Second Person of the Trinity, Jesus Christ, the Eternal Logos made flesh.

SACRED TRADITION

What is Sacred Tradition and Why Do Catholics Believe in It?

Rev. Fr. Gabriel Emeasoba (PhD)

In simple terms, Sacred Tradition is the lived deposit of faith or Gospel, which has been revealed by God, taught by Christ, handed on to the Apostles and preached and preserved by these Apostles and their successors in the Church through all generations till the end of the world. Although God revealed himself in different ways in times past, including through the prophets, the fullness of the Divine revelation was realised in Christ. Hence, when Christ came to the world, he commissioned the Apostles to preach this Goodnews for the salvation of the world (Matthew 28:19-20) —

> *"that in Christ, the fullness of God was pleased to dwell and through him to reconcile all things to God" (Col 1:19-20).*

According to the Catechism of the Catholic Church, the Apostles fulfilled this mandate of Christ in two ways. In the first place, they orally transmitted this Gospel *"by the spoken word of their preaching, by the example they gave, and by the institutions they established"* in the lived experience of the faith within the New Testament communities. Secondly, the Apostles, in concert with other associates within the community of faith, inspired by the Holy Spirit, also committed to writing the message of salvation they received from Christ – Sacred Scripture. However, to preserve the full and living Gospel in the Church, the Apostles appointed successors and bestowed on them teaching authority so that the apostolic preaching, which is expressed in a special way in the Bible will be preserved from one generation to another till the end of the world. It is this living transmission, accomplished in the Holy Spirit that is called Sacred Tradition.

According to the Fathers of the Second Vatican Council, while

> *"Sacred Scripture is the word of God inasmuch as it is consigned to writing under the inspiration of the divine Spirit, Sacred Tradition takes the word of God entrusted by Christ the Lord and the Holy Spirit to the Apostles, and hands it on to their successors in its full purity, so that led by the light of the Spirit of truth, they may in proclaiming it preserve this word of God faithfully, explain it, and make it more widely known."*

Therefore, Catholics believe in Sacred Tradition because they know that *"it is not from Sacred Scripture alone that the Church draws her certainty about everything which has been revealed."* In truth, ever before the Apostles decided to write down the faith they received, they had lived this faith and orally preached it in their communities.

It is indeed within this living Tradition that the canon of the Sacred Scripture was agreed upon, inspired by the Holy Spirit. It is therefore difficult to understand the Scripture or even interpret it outside the context of this lived Tradition within which it was written. Hence, Catholics believe that "Sacred tradition and Sacred Scripture form one sacred deposit of the word of God, committed to the Church." Any account of the revealed word of God which stops with Sacred Scripture is limited.

SACRED TRADITION

Why Do Catholics Use Images Against God's Command?

Rev. Fr. Emmanuel Omokugbo Ojeifo (PhD)

The first of the Ten Commandments given to the people of Israel by God through Moses is often cited as the instance where God prohibited the making or use of graven images:

> *"Do not make for yourselves images of anything in heaven or on earth, or in the water under the earth. Do not bow down to any idol or worship it..." (Exodus 20:4-5).*

We need to understand the context of this command. Israel was going into a territory where they would be surrounded by pagan nations. God wills that they should worship him alone and not be influenced by or flirt with the worship of the pagan deities. In this First Commandment, God establishes himself as the sovereign, the only God worthy of worship.

Yes, God forbade the worship of statues, but he did not forbid the religious use of statues. Instead, he commanded the making of statues and their use in religious contexts. Let us take some examples. In Exodus 25:18-20, God himself commanded Moses to make two cherubs which were to be placed on the two ends of the mercy seat in the Tent of Meeting.

In 1 Chronicles 28:18-19, we read that David gave Solomon the plan

> *"for the altar of incense made of refined gold, and its weight; also, his plan for the golden chariot of the cherubim that spread their wings and covered the ark of the covenant of the Lord. All this he made clear by the writing of the hand of the Lord concerning it all."*

David's plan for the temple included statues of angels. Similarly, Ezekiel 41:17–18 describes graven (carved) images in the idealized temple he was shown in a vision, for he writes, "*On the walls round about in the inner room and [on] the nave were carved likenesses of cherubim.*"

When the Israelites on their journey to the Promised land disobeyed God, God sent fiery serpents to bite them. Following Moses' plea, God commanded him to

> *"make [a statue of] a fiery serpent and set it on a pole; and everyone who is bitten, when he sees it shall live. So, Moses made a bronze serpent and set it on a pole; and if a serpent bit any man, he would look at the bronze serpent and live" (Numbers 21:8–9).*

One had to *look* at the bronze statue of the serpent to be healed, which shows that statues could be used ritually, not merely as religious decorations. In the New Testament, Jesus would cite this instance of the bronze serpent as a prefiguration of his own exodus toward the cross:

> *"Just as Moses lifted up the serpent in the wilderness, so must the Son of Man be lifted up, that everyone who believe in him may have eternal life"* (John 3:14-15).

Religions function by way of mediation. Because we are dealing with infinite and supernatural realities, we need objects to mediate the vast gulf between us, between our minds, and the world of transcendence. This is why virtually all religions have a way of lifting the veil and bridging the gap that separates this immanent world from the transcendent world. Images are representations of reality. Catholics use statues and paintings to recall the person or thing depicted. Even when they pray before a statue, they are not worshipping the statue, just as we would not say that a child who prostrates or bows before an elder (as is done in some indigenous cultures as a sign of respect) is worshipping the elder.

SACRED TRADITION

Why is the Catholic Bible Different From Protestant and Pentecostal Bibles?

Rev. Fr. Gabriel Emeasoba (PhD)

First of all, it must be acknowledged that making a distinction between a Catholic, Protestant or Pentecostal Bible could be confusing. Unfortunately, such distinctions give the impression that there are different Bibles for Catholics, Protestants and Pentecostals. This is not so. There is no confusion in God's Word; ideally, the Word of God is one.

However, how can one explain the fact that while in the so called 'Catholic Bibles', there are 73 books, in the so called 'Protestant Bibles', there are only 66? For the records, Catholics and Protestants have the same 27 books in the New Testament (as defined by St Athanasius in 367) but when it comes to the boundaries of the Old Testament, they differ. While Protestants have 39 books in the Old Testament, Catholics have 46, including seven more books with some additions within shared books. These extra books in the Catholic Bible include **Tobit, Judith, Wisdom of Solomon, Ecclesiasticus / Sirach / Ben Sira, 1–2 Maccabees, Baruch**, and the additions to **Daniel** and **Esther**. While Protestants call these books 'the Apocrypha' (the hidden books), Catholics refer to them as 'Deuterocanonical books.' The word 'deuterocanonical' does not mean that these books are second in authority; they are second only in reception in time as authentic by the Catholic Church.

What one finds is that, while the Protestants stick to the narrow contents of the Hebrew canon (albeit without its sequence of ordering and numbering), Catholics accept these same books plus the deuterocanonical books. The original Hebrew Bible has 24 books. The Protestant Old Testament replicates the same information as the original Hebrew Bible but has organized its contents into 39 books. For example, the Hebrew Bible has one book of Samuel, while the Protestant Bible has I and II Samuel—same book but divided into two parts. On the other hand, the seven extra books of the Catholic Bible (known as the deuterocanonical books) were included into canon of the Bible in the earliest Greek Translation of the Old Testament Hebrew Bible known as the *Septuagint.*

After the deportation of the Jews from Jerusalem, the Jews were forced to abandon their Temple and priests, and with time in exile, they also forgot how to read, write, and speak the Hebrew language. This affected access to the original Hebrew Bible. With Greek later becoming the common language of the time, Jewish scholars decided to translate the Hebrew Scriptures into the Greek language commonly spoken to make it accessible to Jews in foreign communities. It has been held that the 'Septuagint was presumably made for the Jewish community in Egypt when Greek was the common language throughout the region.' However, in composing the Septuagint, the inspired authors added extra 'books of wisdom' and histories about the period in which these later books were written.

These extra books had become widely known and popular by the time of Jesus, and the early Christian writers were familiar with them. Although the New Testament and second-century authors never cite the deuterocanonical books *as scripture*, they do allude to them, showing awareness of them. (See, for example, the allusion to the Jewish martyrs of 2 Maccabees 6–7 in Hebrews 11:35). They were also alluded to in the Pauline epistles. In fact, in the 3rd century AD, 'Christians began to cite the deuterocanonical books as "scripture."' Hence, the Septuagint survived in the early Christian Churches. It was indeed from the Septuagint that St Jerome translated the Old Testament of the Latin translation of the Bible – the Vulgate – in 382 CE.

As a result, in organising the canon of the Bible, while the core Hebrew content the Old Testament was easily accepted as authentic, the status of the extra books continued to be debated in the Church until the Councils of Rome, Florence and Trent, when the Church declared these extra books canonical, hence, deuterocanonical (belonging to the second canon) as against protocanonical books (belonging to the second canon). As already noted, the appellation 'deuterocanonical' only refers to the later acceptance or reception of these books in time. During the Reformation, the Protestants, led by Luther, decided that the additional books which were not in the original Hebrew Bible would not be included in the Christian Bible. This accounts for the differences in the Catholic and Protestant Bible. In the main, the Pentecostals follow the Protestant canon of the Bible.

References

SACRAMENTS:

According to the word The Catechism of the Catholic Church, Sacraments "are efficacious signs of grace, instituted by Christ and entrusted to the Church, by which divine life is dispensed to us. sacraments are the outward signs of inward grace, instituted by Christ to help individuals in their spiritual life and to grow in holiness".

BAPTISM:

*According to the Oration of St. Gregory Nazianzus, Baptism (which in practical term means Immersion – to be buried into Christ's death and to rise with Christ as a new creature) is God's most beautiful and magnificent gift... We call it gift, grace, anointing, enlightenment, garment of immortality, bath of rebirth, seal, and most precious gift. (**The Oration on Holy Baptism,** https://www.newadvent.org/fathers/310240.htm)*

'Baptism is the sacrament of regeneration through water in the word' **(The Catechism of the Catholic Church**, *no. 1213)*

*Go then, to all people everywhere and make them my disciples, baptize them in the name of the Father and of the Son and of the Holy Spirit. (**Good News Translation Bible, Matthew** 28:19)In **Acts** 16:33 the household of the jailer were baptised by the apostles Paul and Silas after he accepted the faith.*

*Joshua says, "As for me and my household, we will serve the Lord." (**New International Version Bible, Joshua** 24:15)*

*"Truly I say to you, unless one is born of water and the spirit, one cannot enter the kingdom of God. What is born of the flesh is the flesh and what is born of the spirit is the spirit... you must be born again. (**New International Version Bible, John** 3:3-7)*

*The sheer gratuitousness of the grace of salvation is particularly manifest in infant baptism. The Church and the parents would deny a child the priceless grace of becoming a child of God were they not to confer Baptism shortly after birth. (**The Catechism of the Catholic Church,** no. 1250)*

HOLY-EUCHARIST:

According to the Catechism of the Catholic Church, the Holy Eucharist is the sacrament of the Body and Blood of Jesus Christ ***(The Catechism of the Catholic Church,*** *no. 1328-1331)*

If the Church allowed those who "are not united" with or in the Church to receive Eucharist, she would seem to be asserting that those who are not in communion with the Church may take part in the very sacrament which definitively marks such communion ***(CTS New Catholics Bible, 1 Corinthians*** *11:27-29).*

The Holy Eucharist or Communion is properly the sacrament of those who are 'in full communion' with the Church. ***(The Catechism of the Catholic Church****, no. 1395)*

The "Eucharist" was first instituted by Jesus Christ during his last supper with his disciples before his death ***(CTS New Catholics Bible, Matthew*** *26:17-29;* ***CTS New Catholics Bible, Mark*** *14:12-25;* ***New International version Bible, Luke*** *22:7-38).*

(The Catechism of the Catholic Church*, no. 1401) Catholic ministers may illicitly administer the sacrament of Eucharist to other baptized non-Catholic Christians who do not have full Communion with the Catholic Church, who cannot approach a minister of their own faith community and on their own ask for it, provided they manifest Catholic faith in this sacrament and are properly disposed"* ***(Code of Canon Law, 844 & 4)***

Unlike other Christian churches, the Catholic Church believes that the Eucharist is the true body and blood of Jesus Christ ***(Good News Translation Bible, Matthew*** *26:26-28,* ***Christian Standard Bible, John*** *6:41-56).*

HOW IS MASS A PRAYER:

The General Instruction of the Roman Missal (No.93) identifies the role of the priest in that as he prays holy Mass, he does so in the person of Christ, he presides over the faithful and proclaims the word of salvation.

The Second Vatican Council explains that the holy mass is the source and summit of our Christian life. The Mass ***(Eucharist meaning thanksgiving)*** *is the greatest prayer we can offer since it is Christ's prayer, Christ's saving sacrifice offered to the heavenly Father for his glory and for our salvation.*

We have affirmation from the mouth of Jesus that there is a possibility of obtaining forgiveness of sins in this age and in the age to come ***(English Standard Version Bible, Matthew*** *12:32).*

CONFIRMATION:

*Jesus promised to send another Advocate from the Father to be with his disciples forever (**New Revised Standard Version Bible, John** 14:16).*

*Holy Baptism is the basis of the whole Christian life, the gateway to life in the Spirit (vitae spiritualis ianua), and the door which gives access to the other sacraments. (**The Catechism of the Catholic Church 1213**) gives the following details about the sacrament of Baptism.*

*Our Lord Jesus Christ also made it part of the evangelization tool for his disciples when commissioning them to make disciples of all nations (**New Revised Standard Version Bible, Matthew** 28:19).*

*Our Lord Jesus Christ received the Holy Spirit at his baptism in the Jordan (**New Revised Standard Version Bible, Matthew** 3:16)*

*The difference between the sacraments of Baptism and Confirmation is a very subtle one in the strict sense because they share a common ground as the Holy Spirit is received; in fact, (**The Catechism of the Catholic Church** no.1285) recommends that.*

*The most significant scriptural reference to the sacrament of Confirmation was the outpouring of the Holy Spirit on the apostles and others on the day of Pentecost as was promised by our Lord Jesus Christ shortly before His ascension into heaven (**New Revised Standard Version Bible, Acts** 1:4-5 & 8).*

*The sacrament of Baptism opens the door to the Christian life. In other words, the first step toward becoming a Christian is receiving the sacrament of Baptism. Our Lord Jesus Christ demonstrated the importance of the sacrament by receiving the Baptism of John (**New Revised Standard Version Bible, Matthew** 3:13-17).*

*There are some scriptural foundations of the sacrament of Confirmation. In the Old Testament, the Prophet Joel in (**New Revised Standard Version Bible, Joel** 2:28-29) talks about God pouring His Spirit upon all flesh in the latter days.*

*We must note first that they form the sacraments of Christian initiation together with the Holy Eucharist. According to the (**Code of the Canon Law 842:1**), Baptism and Confirmation are interrelated and indispensable for full integration into the life of the Church.*

CONFESSION:

A priest is bound to keep the confessional seal **(The Catechism of the Catholic Church**, *no. 1467) even under the pain of death. Any priest that breaks the confessional seal faces automatic (latae sententiae) excommunication* **(Code of Canon Law, 1388 & 1)** *This is one of the most critical aspects of priestly training and the most beautiful dimension of this sacrament.*

According to the **(The Catechism of the Catholic Church**, *no. 976) faith in the forgiveness is associated "not only with faith in the Holy Spirit, but also with faith in the Church and in the communion of saints*

It is a power that is exercised by the priests because of its sacramental nature. This does not preclude the injunction to forgive one another as we recite in Our Lord's Prayer **(Christian Standard Bible, Matthew** *6:12, 14-15).*

In cases of grave speech impediment or illness or lack of common language between the confessor and the penitent. In that case, the interpreter is equally bound to keep the confessional seal **(Code of Canon Law, 983 & 2)**

"No one is prohibited from confessing through an interpreter as long as abuses and scandals are avoided and without prejudice to the prescript of **(Code of Canon Law, 990)**

The practice of sacramental confession among Catholics is grounded in the Scriptures. In the post-resurrection appearance, Jesus said to his disciples: "Receive the Holy Spirit. If you forgive the sins of any, they are forgiven; if you retain the sins of any, they are retained" **(Christian Standard Bible, John** *20:22-23).*

The Catechism goes further to state that through the sacrament of Penance (which is another expression for sacramental Confession), "the baptized can be reconciled with God and with the Church" **(The Catechism of the Catholic Church**, *no. 980)*

The priest does not act on his own accord. He is only but a servant and minister of this sacrament and not the "master of God's forgiveness" **(The Catechism of the Catholic Church**, *no. 1466)*

The priest's absolution; a prayer of thanksgiving and praise and dismissal with the blessing of the priest" **(The Catechism of the Catholic Church**, *no. 1480). Thus, it is quite difficult to effectively exercise this action online without our bodily participation.*

(The Catechism of the Catholic Church, *no. 1482)*

MORTAL SIN AND VENIAL SIN:

*(**The Catechism of the Catholic Church no.**1863) teaches: Venial sin weakens charity; it manifests a disordered affection for created goods; it impedes the soul's progress in the exercise of the virtues and the practice of the moral good; it merits temporal punishment deliberate and unrepented venial sin disposes us little by little to commit mortal sin.*

*(The Catechism of the Catholic Church (1849) says: The distinction between Mortal and Venial sin comes from the First Letter of John (**New Revised Standard Version Bible, 1 John** 5:17), which says, "All wrongdoing is sin, but there is sin that is not mortal."*

*Expanding on the two dimensions of sin, the Catechism of the Catholic Church teaches that sin is Mortal when the object is a "grave matter, committed with full knowledge and deliberate consent" (**Catechism of the Catholic Church no.**1857).*

*Regular and effective confession helps to keep ourselves in check with the evasion of sin in our lives. John's First Letter (**New Revised Standard Version Bible, 1 John** 2:1-2) says: My little children, I am writing this to you so that you may not sin; but if anyone does sin, we have an advocate with the Father, Jesus Christ the righteous; and he is the expiation for our sins, and not for ours only but also for the sins of the whole world.*

*So, we define sin as the transgression of God's laws or commandments (**New Revised Standard Version Bible,1 John** 3:4).*

*The first recorded sin on earth was the disobedience of Adam and Eve (**New Revised Standard Version Bible, Genesis** 3:11).*

*The Ten Commandments (**New Revised Standard Version Bible, Exodus** 20:1-17) give us a perfect example of mortal sin.*

INDULGENCE:

*A plenary indulgence applicable to the dead can be obtained on November 2, the feast of "All Souls". The Catechism while referencing Pope Paul VI's 1967 apostolic constitution, **(Indulgentiarum doctrina no.5),***

*"An indulgence is a remission before God of the temporal punishment due to sins whose guilt has already been forgiven, (**Code of Canon Law**, 992)*

*Any baptized person who seeks plenary indulgence must have the intention of gaining it and must fulfil the prescribed works accordingly (**Code of Canon Law**, 996 & 2), including the three conditions of: Sacramental confession, Eucharistic Communion, and prayer for the intention of the Pope, which may* *be satisfied by reciting one 'Our Father' and one 'hail Mary' or any other prayer freely chosen by the faithful* ***(Indulgentiarum doctrina*** *no.12)* ***(Indulgentiarum doctrina*** *no.7)* ***(Indulgentiarum doctrina*** *no.10)*

As for partial indulgence, one can get that through the devout use of "an object of piety (crucifix, cross, rosary, scapular, or medal) properly blessed by any priest" ***(Indulgentiarum doctrina*** *no.17)*

"Grave sin deprives us of communion with God and therefore makes us incapable of eternal life.... ***(The Catechism of the Catholic Church****, no. 1472)*

He or she must not be under excommunication, and in the state of grace "at least at the end of the prescribed works" ***(Code of Canon Law, 996 &1)***

"The intention of the Church is not just to offer a miraculous act that dispels all punishments due to sin, but to motivate the faithful to "works of devotion, penance, and charity" ***(The Catechism of the Catholic Church****, no. 1478)*

"There are two types of indulgence, namely partial or plenary, which removes respectively either "part or all the temporal punishment due to sin" ***(Code of Canon Law, 993)****. Both forms of indulgence can be gained either for oneself or can be applied to the dead* ***(Code of Canon Law, 994)****, as this is consistent with the Catholic faith in the communion of saints.*

(The Catechism of the Catholic Church, *no. 1475)*

EXTREME UNCTION:

According to St Thomas Aquinas, "...a sacrament properly so called is that which is the sign of some sacred thing pertaining to man; sign of a holy thing so far as it makes men holy." ***(Thomas Aquinas, Summa Theologiae III, q.60, a.2)***

In the New Testament, Christ became the healer of all diseases and infirmities as we read in ***(CTS New Catholic Bible, Mark*** *7:32-36), and in sending out thee Twelve to anoint and heal the sick in* ***(CTS New Catholic Bible, Mark*** *6:13).*

Healing of the sick has been part of our salvific history since it is through disobedience that suffering, sickness and death entered the world ***(English Standard Version Bible, Genesis*** *3:16-19). We see this in the healing of Tobit's blindness in* ***(English Standard Version Bible, Tobith*** *11:15) &* ***(English Standard Version Bible, Wisdom*** *16:12)*

(Catechism of the Catholic Church. 2016.(1131) 267). *London: Catholic Truth Society. Revised Edition.*

(Catechism of the Catholic Church. (1257) 292).

New International Version Bible, Matthew *25:31-46*

Paul Haffner. ***(The Sacramental Mystery).*** *Herefordshire: Gracewing. 2016. 199.*

Sacrament of Anointing of the Sick confers a **Special Grace** *to the person preparing for the journey heavenward.* ***(Catechism of the Catholic Church, no. 1532)***

The New Revised Standard Version. Bangalore: Theological Publications in India. 2003

Vatican Council II: ***(The Conciliar and Post-Conciliar Documents Lumen Gentium:*** *no.14). Edited by Austin Flannery, O.P. Mumbai: St Pauls Press. 1975.*

HOLY ORDERS:

However, the Magisterium documents in 1997 ***(Ecclesiae de Mysterio,*** *Instruction on Certain Questions regarding the Collaboration of the Non-Ordained Faithful in the Sacred Ministry of Priests, Premiss), and most especially the document of the Second Vatican Council, present and clarify the principle of the different identities, the distinction between the common priesthood and the ministerial priesthood.*

In addition to this priesthood and to serve it, there is another form of participation in Christ's mission: the ministry conferred with the Sacrament of Orders or the "ministerial Priesthood". ***(Catechism of the Catholic Church,*** **no. 1591***),*

The ***(Catechism of the Catholic Church,*** **no.1268***) tells us that "by Baptism, (the baptized) share in the priesthood of Christ, in his prophetic and royal mission".*

The liturgy is the action of the whole Mystical Body of Christ, Head, and members ***Sacrosanctum Concilium,*** **no***. 7).*

The second Vatican document of the church ***(Lumen Gentium*** **no.** *10) gives an explicit distinction between the common priesthood and the ministerial priesthood.*

"You will be for me a kingdom of priests and a holy nation." ***Good News Translation Bible Exodus*** *19:6.*

"You, however, are a chosen race, a royal priesthood, a holy nation, a purchased people" ***(Good News Translation Bible 1 Peter*** *2:9)*

MARRIAGE:

It is not necessary to become Catholic, but the Catholic must uphold the obligation to preserve his or her own faith and "ensure the baptism and education of the children in the Catholic Church." **(Catechism of the Catholic Church, no.**1635**).**

*Baptized Catholics in marriages are channels for conveying grace to others. Scripture tells us that the unbelieving spouse is made holy through the believing spouse. (**New International Version Bible 1 Corinthians** 7:14).*

DIVORCE:

***(Catechism of the Catholic Church no.**2386). Divorce and remarriage are serious sins in God's law. We are warned that the unrighteous will not inherit the Kingdom of God.*

***CTS New Catholic Bible, John** 4:17-18, **Malachi** 2:16, **Matthew** 5:31-32, **Matthew** 19:16-19, **Romans** 7:2-3*

*He answered, "Have you not read that he who made them from the beginning made them male and female, and said, "For this reason a man shall leave his father and mother and be joined to his wife, and the two shall become one flesh"? So, they are no longer two but one flesh. What therefore God has joined together, let not man put asunder.' (**King James Version Bible, Matthew** 19:3-10)*

*We are warned that the unrighteous will not inherit the Kingdom of God. Adultery is listed as one of the sins of the unrighteous in (**CTS New Catholic Bible, 1 Corinthians** 6:9- 10)*

SALVATION OUTSIDE CHRIST:

*But without the Church and sacraments Christ has provided as the ordinary means for our sanctification, it is even more difficult. (**English Standard Version Bible, 1 Peter** 4:18)*

*(The **Catechism of the Catholic Church, no.** 830) lays out the truth of the matter succinctly; There is no salvation apart from Christ and his One, Holy, Catholic, and Apostolic Church.*

*(The **Catechism of the Catholic Church, no.** 846-848) "Basing itself on Scripture and Tradition, the Council teaches that the Church, a pilgrim now on earth, is necessary for salvation: the one Christ is the mediator and the way of salvation; he is present to us in his body which is the Church.*

*He says, "He who hears you hears me, and he who rejects you rejects me" (**English Standard Version Bible, Luke** 10:16).*

In ***(English Standard Version Bible, John*** *14:6) Jesus said, "I am the Way, the Truth and the Life, no man can come to the Father except by me." Christ is essential for salvation, and we are saved through the Church.*

It is almighty God who willed "that through the church the manifold wisdom of God might now be made known" ***(English Standard Version Bible, Ephesians*** *3:10). To reject the Church is to reject Christ because it was Christ who gave authority to the Church.*

The bottom line is the straight and narrow road that leads to heaven is not an easy road to begin with ***(English Standard Version Bible, Matthew*** *7:13).*

The Catholic Church teaches that, "extra ecclesiam nulla salus,", "outside the Church there is no salvation." This has its basis in the words of Christ, "Truly I tell you; no one can see the kingdom of God unless they are born again" ***(English Standard Version Bible, John*** *3:3)*

The Church is "the fullness of him who fills all in all" ***(English Standard Version Bible, Ephesians*** *1:23). The Church is Christ in the world.*

PURGATORY:

According to the Catechism: "Sin is before all else an offence against God, a rupture of communion with. At the same time, it damages communion with the Church. ***(Catechism of the Catholic Church. London: Catholic Truth Society. Revised Edition. 2016.*** *no.1440) 329.*

According to him, any builder that does not build on the foundation that is Jesus Christ, will suffer loss, "...will be saved, but only as through fire." ***(English Standard Version Bible, 1 Corinthians*** *3:10-15)*

JosefNeuner,SJandJacquesDupius,SJ. ***(TheChristianFaithintheDoctrinalDocumentsoftheCatholicChurch*** *no.704-711****).*** *EditedbyJacquesDupius.7thEdition. Bangalore: Theological Publications. 2001.*

Joseph Cardinal Ratzinger. ***(Eschatology: Death and Eternal Life 1988. 218).*** *Translated by Michael Waldstein. Washington DC: Catholic university of American Press.*

Joseph Cardinal Ratzinger. ***(Eschatology: Death and Eternal Life. 222-228).*** *The New Revised Standard Version. Bangalore: Theological Publications in India. 2003*

The first biblical foundation in support of the above doctrine is the heroic act of Judas in ***(English Standard Version Bible, 2 Maccabees*** *12:32-45)*

WHY CATHOLICS PRAY FOR THE DEAD AND TO THE DEAD (SAINTS):

About the saints, these are those who "have washed their robes white again in the blood of the Lamb. "That is why the stand before God's throne and serve him day and night in his temple" ***(New International Version Bible, Revelation*** *7:14-17).*

(*Catechism of the Catholic Church,* no. *954***).**

So, there is forgiveness of sins beyond death. The clearest affirmation of this in the Hebrew Scriptures is in ***(New International Version Bible, Maccabees*** *12:38-45).*

The basis of this belief is ***(Good News Translation Bible, Revelation*** *21:27) which speaks of the Heavenly Jerusalem in these terms: "But nothing that is impure will enter the city, nor anyone who does shameful things or tells lies. Only those whose names are written in the Lamb's book of the living will enter the city.*

They have great concern for us because they have communion with us. "Because they are in God's presence, they can plead our cause, just as our guardian angels do" ***(Good News Translation Bible, Matthew*** *18:10).*

We have affirmation from the mouth of Jesus that there is a possibility of obtaining forgiveness of sins in this age and in the age to come ***(Good News Translation Bible, Matthew*** *12:32).*

MARY THE MOTHER OF GOD:

A further testimony to his divinity. It is this divine person, the Logos, who took flesh and dwelt among us ***(New International Version Bible, John*** *1:14), in the womb of the Blessed Virgin Mary.*

An expression that is also repeated at the Transfiguration ***(New International Version Bible,*** *Matt. 17:5)* ***(New International Version Bible,*** *Mk. 9:7)* ***(New International Version Bible,*** *Lk. 9:35)*

New International Version Bible, *2Pet. 1:17). This passage is a solemn revelation of the divine sonship Jesus. Contrary to those who see this term merely as one of endearment, the expression "Son of God" is only used for Jesus in the New Testament.*

At the Baptism at Jordan, a voice from Heaven referred to him saying, "This is my beloved Son in whom I am well pleased" ***(Good News Translation Bible, Matthew*** *3:17)* ***(Good News Translation Bible, Mark*** *1:11)* ***(Good News Translation Bible, Luke*** *3:22)* ***(Good News Translation Bible, John*** *1:34)*

Elizabeth, filled with the Holy Spirit calls her "Mother of my Lord" ***(Good News Translation Bible, Luke*** *1:43).*

Henrici Denzinger, **Enchiridion Symbolorum Definitionum et Declarationum de Robus Fidei et Morum** *(43rd edition), Robert Fastiggi et al, (ed.); (San Francisco: Ignatius Press, 2010), no. 251*

In the Annunciation narrative ***(Good News Translation Bible, Luke*** *1:26-45), she is heavily alluded to by the Angel as one who would give birth to the Son of the Most High* ***(Good News Translation Bible, Luke*** *1:32, 35) and shall name him "Jesus"* ***(Good News Translation Bible, Luke*** *1:31).*

In the **New Testament**, *in Matthew, the birth of Jesus is presented as a fulfilment of this "Emmanuel" passage of Isaiah* ***(English Standard Version Bible, Matthew*** *1:23).*

In the **Old Testament**, *Isaiah foretells of a Virgin who shall "conceive and bear a son and his name shall be called Emmanuel"* ***(English Standard Version Bible, Isaiah*** *7:14).*

Jesus also reveals himself several times as the "I am" ***(English Standard Version Bible, John*** *4:26;* ***English Standard Version Bible, John*** *6:35.*

Ludwig Ott, **Fundamentals of Catholic Dogma**, *James Canon Bastible (ed.), (USA: TAN Books, 1954), 128.*

Nestorius argued that Mary is not the Mother of God because from her was taken the human nature only and not the divine nature of Christ. The Council of Ephesus, in countering this view, maintained that not the nature as such, but the person, Jesus Christ, was conceived and born (Ludwig Ott, **Fundamentals of Catholic Dogma**, *James Canon Bastible (ed.), USA: TAN Books, 1954, 197).*

Scripture scholars often contrast the presentation of Jesus as the "I am" with the identification of God in the burning bush with the same title ***(English Standard Version Bible, Exodus*** *3:14),*

See Second Vatican Council, **Dogmatic Constitution on the Church (Lumen Gentium no.***56-69***)**,

The Catechism of the Catholic Church*, no. 495*

The Nestorian heresy regarded Christ as a human person joined to the divine person of God's son ***(The Catechism of the Catholic Church****, no. 466).*

The only reference to Mary in Pauline writings is in ***(English Standard Version Bible, Galatians*** *4:4: "God sent His Son, born of a woman..." a further testimony to her being the Mother of the divine person, Jesus Christ.*

SACRED TRADITION:

*According to the (**The Catechism of the Catholic Church**, no. 76, section 1, chapter 2, article 2), the apostles fulfilled this mandate of Christ in two ways. In the first place, they orally transmitted this Gospel 'by the spoken word of their preaching, by the example they gave, and by the institutions they established' in the lived experience of the faith within the New Testament communities.*

*According to the (**Second Vatican Council, Dei Verbum,** no. 7) Secondly, the Apostles, in concert with other associates within the community of faith, inspired by the Holy Spirit, also committed to writing the message of salvation they received from Christ – Sacred Scripture.*

*According to the (**The Catechism of the Catholic Church**, no. 78, no. 1) However, to preserve the full and living Gospel in the Church, the Apostles appointed successors and bestowed on them teaching authority so that the apostolic preaching, which is expressed in a special way in the Bible will be preserved from one generation to another till the end of the world. It is this living transmission, accomplished in the Holy Spirit that is called Sacred Tradition.*

*According to the Fathers of the Second Vatican Council, (**Second Vatican Council, Dei Verbum,** no. 9) while 'Sacred Scripture is the word of God inasmuch as it is consigned to writing under the inspiration of the divine Spirit, Sacred Tradition takes the word of God entrusted by Christ the Lord and the Holy Spirit to the Apostles, and hands it on to their successors in its full purity.*

***English Standard Version Bible, Colossians** 1: 19-20 ...that in Christ, the fullness of God was pleased to dwell and through him to reconcile all things to God.*

WHY CATHOLICS USE IMAGES AGAINST GOD'S COMMAND:

*"Do not make for yourselves images of anything in heaven or on earth, or in the water under the earth. Do not bow down to any idol or worship it..." (**Good News Translation Bible, Exodus** 20:4-5).*

*(**Good News Translation Bible, Exodus** 25:18-20) God himself commanded Moses to make two cherubs which were to be placed on the two ends of the mercy seat in the Tent of Meeting.*

*"Just as Moses lifted up the serpent in the wilderness, so must the Son of Man be lifted up, that everyone who believe in him may have eternal life" (**New International Version Bible, John** 3:14-15).*

***(New Catholic Bible, Ezekiel** 41:17–18) describes graven (carved) images in the idealized temple he was shown in a vision, for he writes, "On the walls round about in the inner room and [on] the nave were carved likenesses of cherubim."*

***(New International Version Bible, 1 Chronicles** 28:18-19), we read that David gave Solomon the plan "for the altar of incense made of refined gold, and its weight; also, his plan for the golden chariot of the cherubim that spread their wings and covered the ark of the covenant of the Lord.*

BIBLE:

*A Gaur et al (eds), **'Septuagint Biblical Literature'** (Britannica) https://www.britannica.com/topic/Septuagint For the records, Catholics and Protestants have the same 27 books in the New Testament (as defined by St Athanasius in 367) but when it comes to the boundaries of the Old Testament, they differ. While Protestants have 39 books in the Old Testament, Catholics have 46, including seven more books with some additions within shared books.*

A Guar et al (no 8). It has been held that the 'Septuagint' was presumably made for the Jewish community in Egypt when Greek was the common language throughout the region.

A Guar et al (no 8). Hence, the 'Septuagint' survived in the early Christian Churches. It was indeed from the 'Septuagint' that St Jerome translated the Old Testament of the Latin translation of the Bible — the Vulgate —in 382 CE.

*JD Meade, 'Why are Protestant and Catholic Bibles Different?' **(Text and Canon Institute Phoenix Seminary, 7 November 2021)** https://www.textandcanon.org/why-the-catholic-bible-has-more-books-than-the-protestant-bible/#:~:text=the%20question%20matters. these books 'the Apocrypha' (the hidden books), Catholics refer to them as 'Deuterocanonical books.' The word 'deuterocanonical' does not mean that these books are second in authority; they are second only in reception in time as authentic by the Catholic Church.*

*JD Meade (no 10) Although the New Testament and second-century authors never cite the deuterocanonical books as scripture, they do allude to them, showing awareness of them. (See, for example, the allusion to the Jewish martyrs of **(English Standard Version Bible, 2 Maccabees 6-7**, **English Standard Version Bible, Hebrew** 11:35).*

*MH Sayler, 'Catholic and Protestant Bibles: What is the Difference?' **(Catholic Education Resource Center**, 7 March 2007)*

Manufactured by Amazon.ca
Bolton, ON